The Boss

A Play by Alan Dapré

Series Editors: Steve Barlow and Steve Skidmore

Heinemann

Published by Heinemann Educational Publishers
Halley Court, Jordan Hill, Oxford OX2 8EJ
A division of Reed Educational and Professional Publishing Ltd

OXFORD   MELBOURNE   AUCKLAND
JOHANNESBURG   BLANTYRE   GABORONE
IBADAN   PORTSMOUTH NH (USA)   CHICAGO

First published 2001
05 04 03 02 01
10 9 8 7 6 5 4 3 2 1
ISBN 0 435 21286 9

Illustrations by Andrew Skilleter
Cover Design by Shireen Nathoo Design
Designed by Artistix, Thame, Oxon
Printed and bound in Great Britain by Biddles Ltd

Tel: 01865 888058 www.heinemann.co.uk

Contents

Characters

Jeff King is aged 15. He is big-headed, and calls himself The Boss.

Russ Jones, aged 15, is Jeff's classmate. He ignores Jeff's boasting.

Liz Brown, aged 14, is also in their class. She is Russ's friend.

Rob Newman, aged 15, is a mysterious new boy. He seems very talented.

Father is Rob's dad.
He wants Rob to get
on with everyone else.

Becky is 14. She is very
kind to Rob.

If you perform the play:

Father, in Scenes 2 and 3, could also be played by the
Russ Jones actor.

Becky, in Scene 3, could also be played by the Liz
Brown actor.

S C E N E   O N E

The schoolyard. Jeff throws a basketball at a hoop. He groans as it misses. Jeff throws again and the ball goes in. Liz and Russ enter.

JEFF: Do you want a game?

LIZ: No thanks.

JEFF: *(To Russ)* Liz hates losing.

LIZ: So do you, Jeff.

JEFF: No. I just love winning. You're talking to *The Boss,* remember?

RUSS: *(To Liz)* He thinks he's so perfect.

JEFF: I am. *(Jeff throws the ball towards the basket. It misses)* I meant to do that.

RUSS: Missed by a mile.

JEFF: Well, if you're so good why don't you have a go?

(Jeff passes the ball to Russ.)

RUSS: One try, that's all.

(Russ throws the ball. It goes in.)

LIZ: Good one.

JEFF: Pure luck. Best of three.

RUSS: No. You're right – it was just lucky.

LIZ: I bet that new kid could beat Jeff.

JEFF: What kid?

LIZ: Rob Newman. Becky says he's a fast learner.

JEFF: Oh, him. *(Jeff shrugs)* Wimp. Rob couldn't lift this ball, let alone throw it. *(He throws the ball and it goes in the hoop)* Watch me and weep!

LIZ: Rob could show you up, Jeff.

JEFF: No one beats *The Boss*.

RUSS: Didn't Rob get 100 percent in the science test, Liz?

LIZ: Yeah.

JEFF: Must have seen the answers.

RUSS: What did *The Boss* get?

JEFF: *(Irritated)* More than you two.

LIZ: Eighty-one percent!

JEFF: I had an off day.

RUSS: Sure.

JEFF: You tell this wonder boy of yours that I'm not scared of him.

(Rob enters, carrying a book.)

LIZ: Tell him yourself.

JEFF: Why waste my breath?

RUSS: *(To Rob)* Jeff says he's not scared of you.

ROB: I see. *(Thinks, then smiles)* I am not scared of Jeff.

JEFF: That's fighting talk.

ROB: My father says that fighting is wrong.

JEFF: *(Bored)* So what do you want?

ROB: *(Holding out his hand)* I would like us to be friends.

JEFF: *(Walks away)* Get in line with all the other wannabes.

ROB: *(Looking around)* What others?

RUSS: *(Taking Rob aside)* Don't push your luck, Rob. Jeff has no friends. Jeff is Boss here. He doesn't need friends. Just people who will laugh at his jokes, and do what he says.

ROB: I do not understand.

RUSS: No one understands Jeff, believe me.

ROB: Here is your book, Liz. *(He hands it over)* I read it all when I got home.

LIZ: This thing took me weeks to read!

ROB: *(Smiling)* My father says I have a photographic memory.

JEFF: (Sourly) He would.

RUSS: How far have you got on my chess computer?

ROB: Level 10.

RUSS: That's awesome. My best is level 3.

ROB: I drew my first game then won the rest.

LIZ: How many?

ROB: Fifteen.

RUSS: (To Liz) I only taught him the basic moves.

LIZ: I told you he's a fast learner.

JEFF: (Mocking Rob) Yesterday you were hopeless, and now you're a chess grandmaster. Or lying!

ROB: You sound upset. Do you want to talk about it?

(Jeff scowls. He throws the ball at Rob.)

JEFF: I want you to throw this ball through that hoop.

ROB: *(Pausing for a moment)* I do not know this game.

JEFF: I thought you knew everything.

ROB: School is over. I must go.

JEFF: Three throws, that's all. Think of it as a challenge. Whoever wins is the boss.

ROB: I am unable to take part in your challenge. I have books to take back to the library.

(Rob drops the ball and exits.)

JEFF: See? He can't handle the pressure. I'm boss, right? He walked away.

LIZ: He had to go.

JEFF: Why – because Daddy says?

LIZ: If Rob had won your challenge, would you really let him be *The Boss*?

JEFF: What do you think? *(Jeff bounces the ball across the stage)* It doesn't make sense, the way your friend becomes so good at things – overnight.

RUSS: Maybe he's a genius?

JEFF: *(Pause)* Yeah, and I'm a brain surgeon.
(To Russ) What school did he go to before this one?

RUSS: No one knows.

LIZ: Rob never talks about his past.

JEFF: It's as if he never had one. *(Jeff pauses, then smiles)* I think someone ought to see where this genius of yours lives.

RUSS: *(To Jeff)* Count me out. Why can't you leave Rob alone?

JEFF: I want to see what makes him tick, that's all. It's not a crime.

(He exits.)

RUSS: I wouldn't want Jeff snooping round my house.

LIZ: I'll warn Rob. The library is on my way home.

RUSS: See you tomorrow.

LIZ: Sure.

(Liz exits. Russ walks off the other way.)

SCENE TWO

Inside Rob's house. Rob's father opens the door and comes inside, followed by Jeff. The room is packed with hi-tech gadgets and equipment.

FATHER: I'm sorry about the mess. We don't get many visitors. Would you care for a drink?

(Jeff shakes his head.)

JEFF: You've got some amazing gear here.

(Jeff picks up a small metal object.)

FATHER: I'd rather you didn't touch that. It's the only one of its kind.

JEFF: *(Puts it back)* What is it?

FATHER: Priceless.

JEFF: Oh. *(Looks around)* Have you lived here long?

FATHER: Ten years or so.

JEFF: What was the name of Rob's old school?

FATHER: *(Edgy)* My wife taught him at home. *(Pause)* When she died last year I thought it best to send Rob to school.

JEFF: So he could make friends.

FATHER: Yes.

(Jeff smirks.)

JEFF: We're in the same tutor group. In fact, we're *such* good friends I was thinking of inviting Rob round to my house for tea.

FATHER: *(Alarmed)* My son only eats at home … he needs a special diet. *(He looks at his watch.)* Rob had to go to the library. He should be back soon.

JEFF: I'd better be going.

FATHER: Shall I tell Rob you called?

JEFF: No. *(Smirking)* I'll tell him tomorrow.

(They walk to the door, just as Liz and Rob enter. Rob can hardly stand.)

LIZ: I found Rob like this in the library. He was slumped over his books.

(Father helps Rob to sit down.)

JEFF: What's up with him?

LIZ: I don't know. It could be a virus.

ROB: *(Weakly)* Jeff, what are you doing here?

JEFF: *(Lying)* I was just passing. I thought I'd drop in, seeing as we're such good friends.

ROB: Friends?

JEFF: Yeah.

ROB: But I thought…

FATHER: It's time you rested, Robert.

ROB: I'll go to my room. *(Rob exits)* I need to recharge my batteries.

FATHER: *(Edgy)* He's tired, that's all. Thank you for bringing my son home.

LIZ: No problem.

JEFF: He looks run down.

FATHER: *(Sharply)* Robert is fine! You'll see him at school tomorrow.

JEFF: Good. *(To Liz, but so Father can hear)* Ready for his challenge, I hope.

LIZ: Jeff!

FATHER: What challenge?

JEFF: I challenged Rob to a basketball shootout but he chickened out.

FATHER: My son doesn't play basketball. I haven't taught him the game.

JEFF: That's too bad.

LIZ: Jeff. You're out of order. Rob is in no state to do anything at the moment.

FATHER: (Serious) My son has remarkable powers of recovery. He will be ready tomorrow.

LIZ: So the challenge is on?

FATHER: Yes. It will be a good test for Robert.

JEFF: (He looks at Liz smugly) Sorted!

LIZ: Time for us to go, Jeff.

JEFF: Better practise my dunking.

LIZ: (To Jeff) You couldn't dunk a biscuit.

JEFF: I can do anything! I'm *The Boss*.

LIZ: So you keep saying.

JEFF: Rob has no chance. *(To Liz, but so Father can hear)* The old man can't work miracles.

(They exit. Father smiles.)

FATHER: Maybe not – but I can build them.

(Father walks over to a desk and picks up a screwdriver. He exits.)

SCENE THREE

The schoolyard. Becky enters to see Rob staring up at the basket. He is holding a basketball.

BECKY: What are you doing?

ROB: I am calculating the flight of the ball. *(He nods)* It is done.

BECKY: Liz told me about the challenge. I didn't know if you would go ahead with it.

ROB: My father wants me to. He says it will be a good test.

BECKY: What do you want?

ROB: What I want is not important.

BECKY: Don't you want to win Jeff's challenge?

ROB: If I win I win.

BECKY: *(Amazed)* How can you be so cool? You're up against *The Boss*.

ROB: My father says he is only human.

(Jeff enters, holding a CD player.)

JEFF: Enter… *The Boss*.

(Jeff struts around the stage.)

BECKY: Good luck, Rob.

JEFF: He'll need it. Do you want to go first or second?

ROB: Second.

(Rob throws the ball at Jeff. The force knocks Jeff backwards.)

JEFF: Playing tough, eh? *(Jeff switches off the music)* Let the challenge begin. Best of three. *(Jeff throws the ball. It goes in)* Easy!

(Rob picks up the ball. He looks up at the hoop and throws. He scores.)

BECKY: One all.

JEFF: Fluke.

(Jeff throws and again the ball goes in. He punches the air. Rob calmly takes his turn and scores.)

BECKY: Two all!

(Jeff is irritated. He throws and the ball misses the hoop. Rob picks the ball up. He looks at Jeff who scowls.)

BECKY: This to win.

(As Rob throws, Jeff nudges him in the back.)

JEFF: Pathetic. What a miss!

BECKY: I can't believe you did that!

JEFF: *(Coldly)* The Boss doesn't lose.

BECKY: You didn't win either! It's a draw.

JEFF: Who says the challenge is over? It's in two parts. One physical … one mental.

BECKY: You're making this up as you go along.

JEFF: What do you expect? *(Smug)* I am *The Boss.* Part two is very simple. *(To Rob)* I ask you a question on anything I like. Then you can ask me one.

BECKY: Rob should go first.

JEFF: I'm first. We're playing by my rules.

ROB: I am ready. Ask your question.

JEFF: *(Grinning)* What word rhymes with orange?

BECKY: That isn't fair.

JEFF: Answer the question, Rob.

ROB: I am searching my memory.

JEFF: And?

ROB: And I… and I…

BECKY: Rob, you don't have to answer this.

JEFF: He does.

(Rob begins to move jerkily. He falls down.)

ROB: Nothing rhymes with orange.

JEFF: Nothing… orange. They don't rhyme.

ROB: But… but…

BECKY: Rob!

(Father enters. He sees Rob on the ground and runs over.)

FATHER: *(To Jeff)* What have you done?

JEFF: I asked him a question, that's all.

ROB: I... I...

FATHER: This is my fault. I should have known he wasn't ready for school!

BECKY: Is Rob all right?

FATHER: He'll be fine, but I think you'd better go.

(Becky nods. Jeff starts to move away.)

FATHER: Not you!

BECKY: *(To Rob)* I'll see you later.

(Becky exits.)

ROB: *(Smiles)* Bec...ky...

FATHER: What exactly did you say to my son?

JEFF: What word rhymes with orange? It was just a question … part of the challenge.

(*Panicking*) I just wanted to see what he was made of.

FATHER: Really. In that case, why don't I show you?

(*He takes a screwdriver and opens a panel in the back of Rob's head. Rob freezes. Jeff is shocked.*)

FATHER: These are Rob's logic circuits. Your trick question has caused them to short-circuit.

JEFF: That's… that's…

FATHER: Shocking, isn't it?

JEFF: Rob is a robot?

FATHER: Oh, he's more than that. In some ways he's more human than a human. My son is programmed to show love and forgiveness.

JEFF: (*Stammering*) How can… it… be your son?

FATHER: I created Robert. He is part of me. My wife and I wanted a child. But it was impossible.

So I decided to create something – someone – perfect.

(Jeff kneels next to Rob.)

FATHER: It had never been done before.

JEFF: This is awesome. *(He touches Rob's face)* So lifelike, it's unreal.

FATHER: Oh, he's real enough. It was a challenge, but I wouldn't give up.

JEFF: You sound like me.

FATHER: I was like you. Once. Always wanted to be the best.

JEFF: The Boss! The others look up to me. Liz, Russ. Becky.

(Father sighs. He probes the back of Rob's head with the screwdriver.)

FATHER: They see through you. Especially Becky. She cares more about this pile of plastic and metal than you. You're no boss. Just someone who likes to think he is.

JEFF: I don't need them.

FATHER: We all need friends. *(He closes the panel)*
             Right now, Rob could do with one.

JEFF: It's a robot.

FATHER: Rob doesn't know that. *(Sadly)* One day he
             will realise that he's not the same as the rest
             of us.

JEFF: How?

FATHER: My son never gets any older. He can't eat or
             drink. One day he will work out why. *(Pause)*
             Sometimes I wonder if I did the right thing.
             Did I have the right to play God?

JEFF: You can't change things. *(Pause)* He's here,
             like it or not.

FATHER: He's not perfect.

JEFF: No one's perfect. *(Pause)* Not even me.

FATHER: Do your friends know?

JEFF: I don't have any.

FATHER: You do.

(They both look at Rob. Jeff nods.)

JEFF: He's coming round.

(Rob's eyes open.)

ROB: Father.

FATHER: *(Smiling)* Son.

JEFF: *(Holding out his hand)* Friend?

(Rob grasps it. Jeff begins to lead him offstage. Father stands, watching them go.)

ROB: Please… no more challenges.

JEFF: Sure whatever you say, Rob. *(Pause)* You're the boss.

(Fade to blackout.)